YOU ARE
Beautiful

Beauty is not just in the face; it is a light in your heart.

Happiness always looks beautiful on you!

Kindness makes you the most beautiful person in the world, no matter what you look like.

Give your body and skin a tune up.
Luxury is not as important as maintenance.

Your skin is your best accessory. Take good care of it.

Generously apply the oil of refined politeness.

Mirror, mirror on the wall, who is the fairest of them all? You, so gentle and kind, You, with a beautiful mind.

Wisdom is like flowers in your hair. It will beautify your life.

LOOK FOR THE BEAUTY IN EVERYDAY THINGS AND YOU WILL BE BEAUTIFUL.

Kind words and loving thoughts, kind acts done in a joyful way are your greatest beauty.

The beauty of kindness and manners will help you fit in anywhere.

There is no
specific age
for beauty.
You can
be beautiful
no matter
what age
you are.

Fashion can be fun! Mix and match to enhance your natural beauty.

Don't just go by how you look in your clothes, but by how you feel in them.

We don't have to all look the same. We don't have to try to be super models. Being YOU is your greatest beauty.

Beauty from the inside reveals itself in love, joy, peace, gentleness and kindness. That is the most attractive beauty of all.

The best and most beautiful things in the world cannot be seen or even touched, they must be felt with the heart.

Keeping your body in good health is the best way to keep your mind strong and beautiful.

Very often a girl's beauty is most apparent in what she chooses NOT to say. Think before you speak.

Beauty is about being the best version of yourself, inside and out.

Make every decision pass through a filter of beauty. What you wear, how you spend your time, who you let into your life, or what you say (or don't say).

Taking care of yourself in big ways and small ways will help you reap beautiful results.

Don't try to be someone you're not. Instead, focus on fully developing who you are.

You don't have to be perfect. Often it's through your imperfections that you gain character, depth and charm.

If you are sure of who you are on the inside, you will appear confident and sure of yourself on the outside.

Texts: Agnes de Bezenac.
Illustrations: Agnes de Bezenac
Cover coloring: Jackson
Proofreading: iCharacter team and Martine Caroni
Published by iCharacter Limited ®. (Ireland)
Kidible is an imprint of icharacter Ltd.
Copyright 2019 iCharacter Limited

Copyright © 2019 by iCharacter Limited ®. All rights reserved. No part of this book may be reproduced in any form or by any electronic or mechanical means, including information storage and retrieval systems, without written permission from the publisher or author, except in the case of a reviewer, who may quote brief passages embodied in critical articles or in a review.

About the author

Agnes lives with her husband and 2 children in a small town in the country side of France. Agnes has a heart for children and young teenage girls. She spends most of her waking hours writing, drawing and creating books and material that bring values and educational topics to life in a variety of fun ways.

In her spare time she enjoys walking, having fun with her kids, cooking and decorating. One of her greatest joys is to see kids enjoying and learning with her books, games and activities.

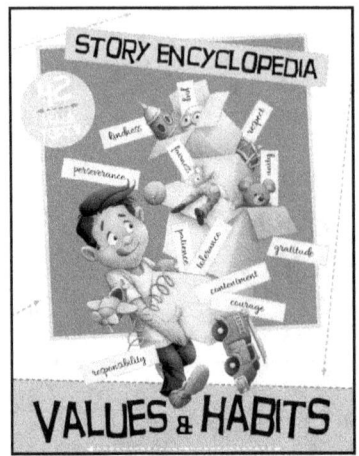

www.kidible.eu

www.ingramcontent.com/pod-product-compliance
Lightning Source LLC
Chambersburg PA
CBHW070137080526
44586CB00015B/1729